W9-AHY-588

J
597.96
Bar
Bargar
Rat snakes

R520115
6.50

DATE DUE			

SK

GREAT RIVER REGIONAL LIBRARY
St. Cloud, Minnesota 56301

RAT SNAKES

THE SNAKE DISCOVERY LIBRARY

Sherie Bargar   Linda Johnson

Photographer/Consultant: George Van Horn

R 520115

S248919

Watermill Press

Mahwah, New Jersey

© 1987 Rourke Enterprises, Inc.

All rights reserved. No part of this book
may be reproduced or utilized in any form
or by any means, electronic or mechanical
including photocopying, recording or by any
information storage and retrieval system
without permission in writing from the
publisher.

Library of Congress Cataloging in Publication Data

Bargar, Sherie, 1944-
   Rat snakes.

   (The Snake discovery library)
   Includes index.
   Summary: Discusses the harmless rat snake, which
benefits farmers by devouring thousands of rats
each year.
   1. Elaphe—Juvenile literature.   2. Snakes—
Juvenile literature.   [1. Rat snakes.   2. Snakes]
I. Johnson, Linda, 1947-   .   II. Van Horn,
George, ill.   III. Title.   IV. Series: Bargar,
Sherie, 1944-   .   Snakes discovery library.
QL666.O636B38   1987   597.96   87-12796
ISBN 0-86592-247-0

Title Photo:
Red Rat Snake
Elaphe guttata

TABLE OF CONTENTS

RAT SNAKES

The shiny rat snakes are members of the *Colubridae* family, the largest family of snakes in the world. These unique snakes are 4 to 5 feet long as adults. The **nonvenomous** rat snakes are constrictors. Many of the species are tree dwellers. Even if they live on the ground, they are notoriously good tree climbers.

Red Rat Snake
Elaphe guttata

WHERE THEY LIVE

Deserts, prairies, farms, forests, and other wooded areas provide homes for rat snakes. They search the **burrows** of other animals and climb trees to find **prey**. They are able to climb wooden rafters in barns and deserted buildings. Rat snakes inhabit every continent except Australia. Most American Rat Snakes live east of the Rocky Mountains.

Typical Red Rat Snake Habitat

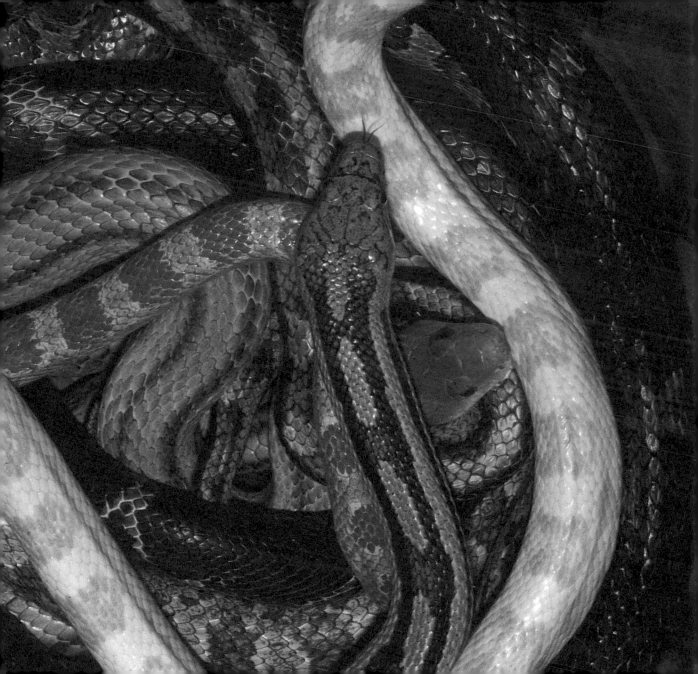

HOW THEY LOOK

The slim, muscular rat snake may have one of many different color patterns. Their shiny, **keeled** scales may be a solid color, blotched, or striped. Their strong bodies average 5 feet in length. The snake's head is a distinct part of its body, and its tail is tapered. The belly of the snake is flat. A cross section of the snake would look very much like a loaf of bread being rounded at the top and resting solidly on a flat bottom.

9

THEIR SENSES

The most important sense for the rat snake is smell. The snake flicks out its tongue to survey the particles in the air. A sample of the surrounding particles is taken by the tongue to the Jacobson's organ in the roof of its mouth. The particles are **analyzed** there to identify what is nearby. The rat snake's vision detects movement near it. Locating and identifying the source of movement helps the rat snake seize its prey. Since the rat snake is a tree dweller, the sense of **vibration** is only useful when it travels or rests on the ground.

Gulf Hammock Rat Snake
Elaphe obsoletta williamsi

Yellow Rat Snakes
Elaphe quadriuittata

Yellow Rat Snake
Elaphe quadriuittata

THE HEAD AND MOUTH

The distinctly large head of the rat snake has two big eyes. There are no fangs in the rat snake's mouth. Instead, there are sharp, curved, needle-like teeth which are used for gripping and holding its **prey**. There are 4 rows of teeth in the roof of the mouth and 1 row of teeth on each side of the lower jaw. The teeth are used to position the **prey** in its mouth. The windpipe extends from the throat to the mouth. The extended windpipe allows the snake to breathe while its entire mouth is filled with **prey**.

Siberian Rat Snake
Elaphe shrenki

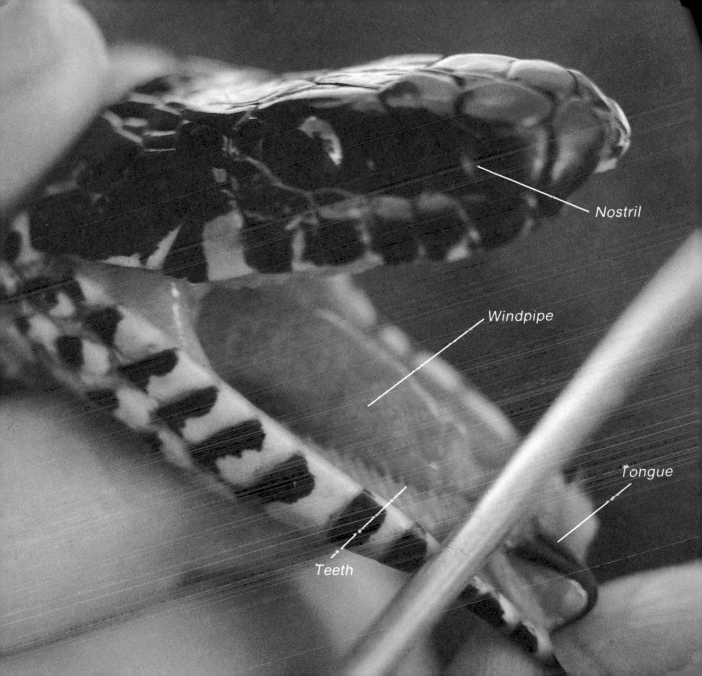

Nostril

Windpipe

Tongue

Teeth

BABY RAT SNAKES

In spring or autumn, female rat snakes lay between 5 and 30 eggs in decayed vegetation or hollow logs. In about 10 weeks, 12-inch babies hatch. Most young snakes have a blotched pattern and often this pattern changes to a solid or striped pattern as they mature. Some species retain their blotched markings. From birth, the babies can kill **prey** and take care of themselves.

Yellow Rat Snake with Baby
Elaphe quadriuittata

PREY

Being an active hunter, the rat snake is ready to attack **prey** day or night. The rat snake eats birds and their eggs, small animals, rats, and mice. The **prey** is snatched from tree branches, animal **burrows**, or off the ground. The rat snake kills its **prey** by wrapping its body around a small animal. Each time the animal breathes out, the snake tightens its hold around the chest. This keeps the small animal from being able to breathe. This method of killing **prey** is constriction.

Siberian Rat Snake feeding
Elaphe shrenki

THEIR DEFENSE

Camouflage is a key element in the rat snake's defense. Hidden in its natural environment, the rat snake is unnoticed by most potential enemies. If the enemy draws too near, the rat snake responds rapidly. It bites to protect itself. To warn the unwelcome **intruder**, the rat snake rattles its tail against the leaves or surrounding surfaces. Although the snake cannot hear the warning sound it makes, the **intruder** should be aware of its presence and danger. Ignoring this warning causes the rat snake to attack.

Gulf Hammock Rat Snake
Elaphe obsoletta williamsi

RAT SNAKES AND PEOPLE

People should not fear the harmless rat snake. As a matter of fact, rat snakes are beneficial to farmers because they devour thousands of rats each year. If the rats were not eaten by these snakes, crops would be destroyed by the huge population of rats. Rat snakes are beautiful because of their many colorful patterns. Their beauty is one of the reasons that they are popular pets. Rat snakes thrive in captivity and are very interesting snakes to observe.

GLOSSARY

analyze (AN a lyze) analyzed — To find out what something is.

burrow (BUR row) burrows — A hole dug in the ground by an animal for its home.

camouflage (CAM ou flage) — The color of an animal's skin that matches the ground around it.

intruder (in TRUD er) intruders — One who approaches another and is not welcome.

keel (KEEL) keeled — A ridge down the middle.

nonvenomous (non VEN om ous) — Not harmful.

prey (PREY) — An animal hunted or killed by another animal for food.

vibrate (VI brate) vibration -— To move back and forth.

INDEX